2 MEN IN THE TEMPLE

LUKE 18:9-14 FOR CHILDREN

Written by Joann Scheck
Illustrated by Jim Roberts

CONCORDIA

ARCH Books

MANUFACTURED IN THE UNITED STATES OF AMERICA

ISBN 0-570-06036-2

One afternoon in Palestine
a tax collector locked his door.
His greedy fingers soon untied
his money bag. He looked inside
and spilled the gold upon the floor.
"And now, before I send the king
his taxes," laughed the little man,
"I'd better keep a few for me.
Let's see, shall I keep one—two—three?
Why not keep all the gold I can?"

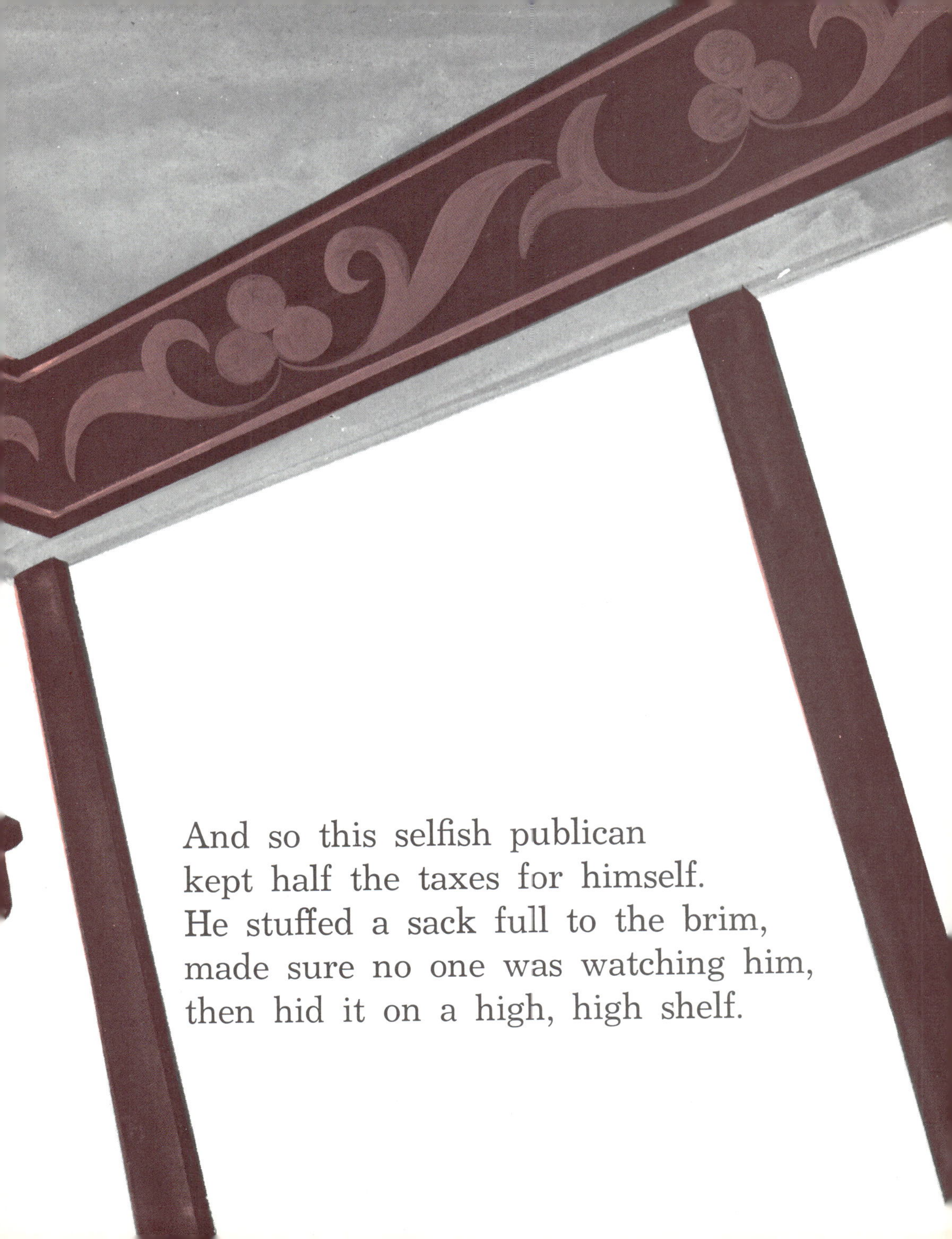

And so this selfish publican
kept half the taxes for himself.
He stuffed a sack full to the brim,
made sure no one was watching him,
then hid it on a high, high shelf.

That afternoon in Palestine
another man went to his door.
He opened it and left it wide
so passers-by could look inside
and see him kneeling on the floor.
They heard this man—the Pharisee—
call out aloud to God in prayer.
For many hours he prayed and praised,
and all that heard were quite amazed;
such holy men are surely rare!

At dinnertime the Pharisee
and all his family sat to eat.
His wife had cooked a lovely meal
of home-baked bread and tender veal
and several other kinds of meat.
But all the Pharisee would do
was pass the food and shake his head.
"I only want to fast and pray.
I'll not eat anything today
except for water and for bread."

Now later on the publican
went out his door to walk a bit
when suddenly he heard a cry:
"You are a thief! You cheat and lie!
This time you won't get by with it!"
An angry crowd began to push
and pull the little man about.
The tax collector shook with fear
to see some men with sticks come near.
He'd soon be dead, without a doubt.

But just that moment soldiers came
and quickly chased the crowd away.
The publican was free at last;
he turned and ran back home quite fast
and didn't leave again all day.

Outside his door he met three men
who begged for money by the way.
"Come," the Pharisee called out
(so all his neighbors heard his shout),
"here's something for you three today!"

Meanwhile the Pharisee walked by,
pretending not to hear or see.
While shouts and screams had filled the air,
his head was bowed as if in prayer.
But he was watching secretly.
"Too bad," he grumbled to himself.
"Too bad the publican got free.
Now I must hurry right along
and get back home where I belong,
for night is coming, I can see."

Again that night the Pharisee
ate only water and some bread.
"How very happy God must be
to have a friend as good as me,"
he thought as he climbed into bed.

Across the town the publican
was also lying in his bed.
He tossed and turned the whole long night.
He knew the people had been right,
and guilty thoughts buzzed through his head.
"I *am* a cheat. I *am* a thief.
The things they said are true, I know.
How very sorry now I feel
that I began to lie and steal.
What can I do? Where shall I go?"

Next day the sorry publican
went to the temple in despair.
He tiptoed quietly inside,
stepped back behind a post to hide,
then all alone he bowed in prayer.

The Pharisee moved far away,
stood straight and tall, and felt quite proud.
"How better off the world would be
if all the people were like me,"
he thought as he prayed out aloud,
"O Lord, I thank You that I'm not
like other wicked, sinful men.
I fast while others eat their fill;
I give gifts to the poor and ill.
You know how very good I've been.
I thank You that I'm not like him—
that lying, cheating publican!"

Meanwhile the publican still prayed.
He beat his chest; he looked dismayed,
so sorry for the things he'd done.
His eyes looked down upon the ground.

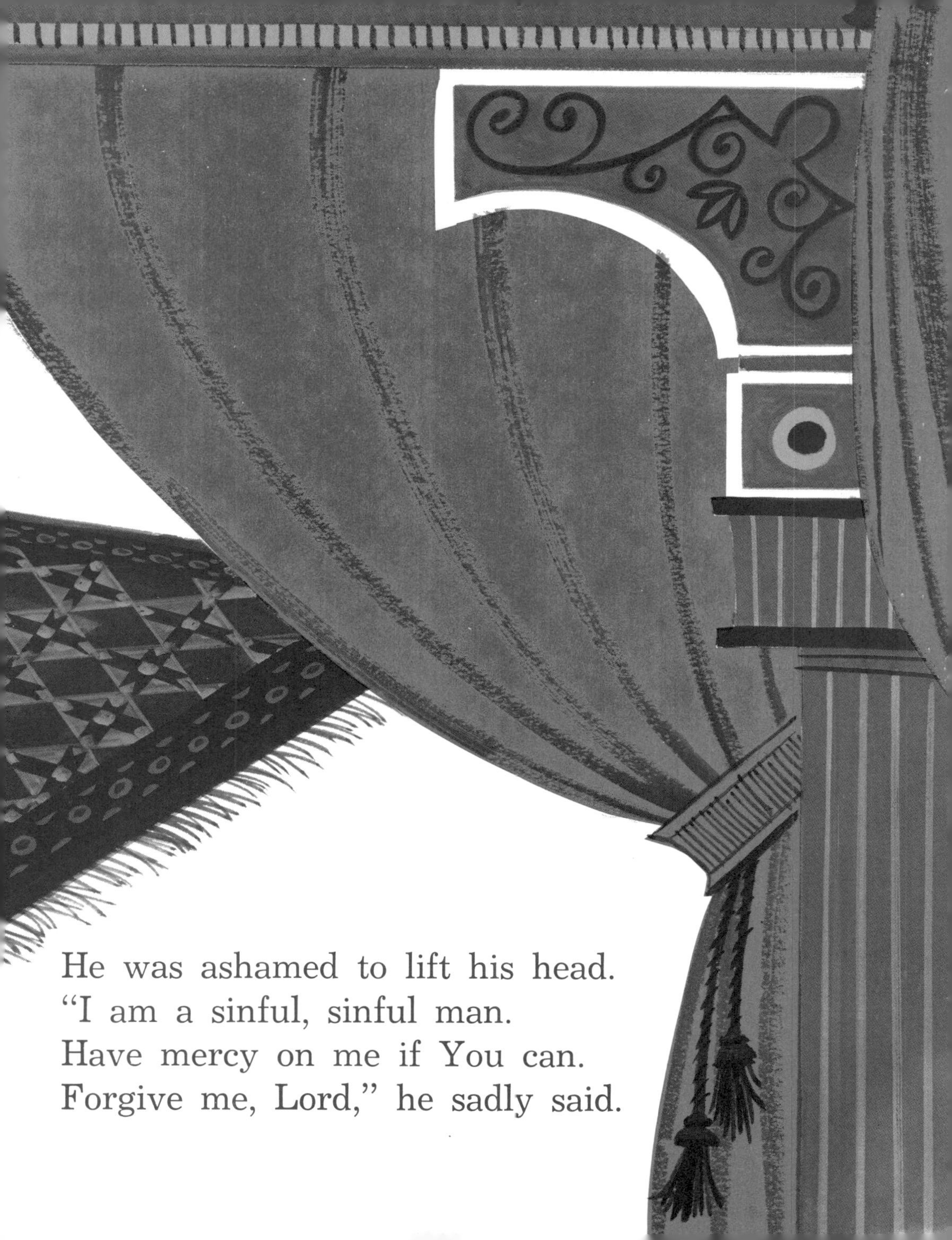

He was ashamed to lift his head.
"I am a sinful, sinful man.
Have mercy on me if You can.
Forgive me, Lord," he sadly said.

Then suddenly the publican
became as happy as could be.
"Oh, thank You, thank You, Lord!" he cried.
"I feel so very good inside.
Oh, thank You for forgiving me!"
The publican went out the door,
and down the street he gaily ran.
He quickly got his money sack
and gave the stolen gold all back.
Then he went home a happy man.

Dear Parents:

We understand the point of this story if we remember that Jesus "told this parable to some who trusted in themselves that they were righteous and despised others" (Luke 18:9). They are like the Pharisee who paraded his piety in the temple and despised the tax collector. The prayer of the Pharisee failed because he lacked humble trust in the merciful goodness of God.

Far off in the corner stood the publican, a sorrowful penitent in great need of forgiveness. He was a thief, and he knew it. He had no record of good deeds to offer. All he could do was cast himself on the mercy of God.

Jesus comments, "I tell you, this man [the publican] went down to his house justified rather than the other" (Luke 18:14). God forgives those who trust in His mercy, not those who are proud of their actions.

This parable speaks to children as well as adults. Have you noticed how easily children express pride in their actions and superiority over less fortunate children? You can help your child recognize these feelings and lead him to be confident that God is merciful and forgiving in Jesus Christ.

The Editor